Contents

Any words appearing in the text in bold, **like this**, are explained in the Glossary.

The seasons

In some parts of the world, the **year** consists of two seasons – a dry season and a rainy season. In central Australia, the Aborigines divide their year into five seasons. For most of us, though, the year is made up of four seasons: **spring**, **summer**, **autumn** and **winter**.

The importance of the seasons

The things we do are influenced by the seasons. This was particularly true in the past when more people worked on the land. In spring, new lambs are born. Towards the end of the summer, wheat, corn and other crops are harvested. In the autumn and winter, the fields are ploughed and made ready for replanting.

Lambs are born in the spring.

The Heinemann English Guide to the Seasons

Graham Dolan

Royal Observatory Greenwich

www.heinemann.co.uk
Visit our website to find out more information about Heinemann Library books.

To order:
 Phone 44 (0) 1865 888066
Send a fax to 44 (0) 1865 314091
 Visit the Heinemann Bookshop at www.heinemann.co.uk to browse our catalogue and order online.

First published in Great Britain by Heinemann Library, Halley Court, Jordan Hill, Oxford OX2 8EJ, a division of Reed Educational and Professional Publishing Ltd. Heinemann is a registered trademark of Reed Educational & Professional Publishing Ltd.

OXFORD MELBOURNE AUCKLAND JOHANNESBURG BLANTYRE
GABORONE IBADAN PORTSMOUTH (NH) USA CHICAGO

Designed by Celia Floyd
Illustrations by Jeff Edwards
Originated by Dot Gradations, UK
Printed in Hong Kong/China

05 04 03 02 01
10 9 8 7 6 5 4 3 2 1
ISBN 0 431 13001 9 (hardback)

06 05 04 03 02
10 9 8 7 6 5 4 3 2 1
ISBN 0 431 13005 1 (paperback)

British Library Cataloguing in Publication Data

Dolan, Graham
The Greenwich Guide to the seasons
1. Seasons – Juvenile literature
I. Title II. The seasons
525.5

Acknowledgements
The Publishers would like to thank the following for permission to reproduce photographs: Pg.4 Still Pictures; Pg.5 PhotoDisc; Pg.12 National Maritime Museum; Pg.13 National Maritime Museum; Pg.19 Oxford Scientific Films; Pg.20 NHPA; Pg.21Bruce Coleman Collection; Pg.22 Oxford Scientific Films; Pg.23 [top] Bruce Coleman Collection [bottom] Oxford Scientific Films; Pg.24 Science Photo Library; Pg.25 Science Photo Library; Pg.26 Oxford Scientific films; Pg.27 Oxford Scientific Films; Pg 28 Bruce Coleman Collection; Pg.29 Bruce Coleman Collection.

Cover photograph reproduced with permission of PhotoDisc.

Spine logo reproduced with permission of the National Maritime Museum.

Every effort has been made to contact copyright holders of any material reproduced in this book. Any omissions will be rectified in subsequent printings if notice is given to the Publisher.

When we go on holiday, what we do, and where we go, often depends on the time of year. We usually go on beach holidays in the summer, when the weather is warmer. Skiing holidays are usually taken in the winter, when the weather is colder and there is snow on the ground.

Summer holidays at the seaside.

But why do the seasons occur? And why are they repeated from one year to the next? Why is it summer in Australia when it is winter in Europe and North America? The answers to these questions lie in the way in which the Earth **orbits** the Sun.

Our moving Earth

The Sun is our nearest star. It gives us light and **energy**. The Earth moves around the Sun. This movement, or **orbit**, affects our **years**, seasons and **days**.

As the Earth goes on its journey, we pass from one season to the next. The pattern of the seasons repeats itself each time the Earth begins a new orbit. Our year is based on this repeating pattern. The pattern repeats itself roughly every $365\frac{1}{4}$ days.

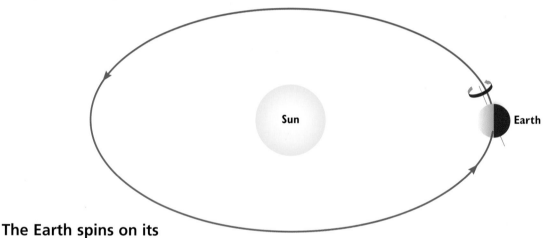

The Earth spins on its axis just over 365 times in the time that it takes to orbit the Sun once.

Day and night

Our Earth is also spinning on its own **axis**. When the part of the Earth that we are on faces the Sun, we receive light and energy. We call it **daytime**. As the Earth spins, we eventually end up facing away from the Sun. When this happens, light and energy from the Sun can no longer reach us. It goes dark and night begins.

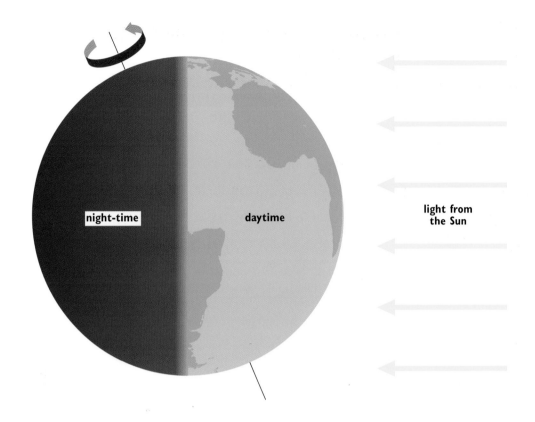

night-time

daytime

light from
the Sun

When it is daytime
on one side of the Earth,
it is **night-time** on the other.

Long and short days

We say that the days in **winter** are shorter than they are in **summer**, but we don't mean that the days themselves are shorter. Each day is always 24 hours long. Instead, we mean that there are fewer hours of daylight each day and more hours of darkness. This happens because the Earth leans as it orbits the Sun.

Our leaning Earth

As the Earth makes its journey around the Sun, it leans at an angle. This affects the length of our **days** and the height at which the Sun appears in the sky. It causes the seasons to occur.

As the Earth moves around its **orbit**, the direction in which it leans scarcely changes. On one side of its orbit, around June, the Earth's North Pole points towards the Sun. On the opposite side of its orbit, around December, the North Pole points away from the Sun.

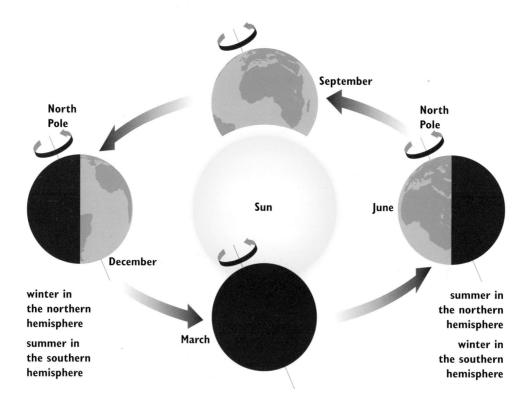

September

North Pole

North Pole

Sun

June

December

winter in the northern hemisphere

summer in the southern hemisphere

March

summer in the northern hemisphere

winter in the southern hemisphere

The Earth always leans in the same direction as it orbits the Sun.

Summer and winter

When the North Pole points towards the Sun, people north of the **tropics** get warmer weather – they have their **summer**. When it points away from the Sun, they get colder weather – they have their **winter**.

When the North Pole points towards the Sun, there are more hours of daylight each day, and the Sun rises higher in the sky. More **energy** is received and it is hotter.

In countries south of the tropics, summer occurs when the South Pole points towards the Sun. This happens when the North Pole is pointing away from the Sun.

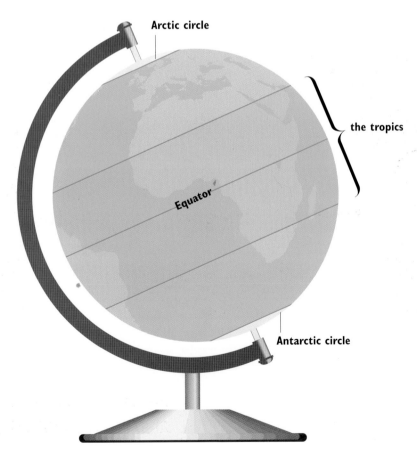

Arctic circle

the tropics

Equator

Antarctic circle

The tropics cover the areas of the Earth on either side of the Equator.

The effect of the Earth's lean

The changing length of the day

In Britain the **days** are longer in the **summer**, because the Earth is leaning on its **axis**. This part of the Earth, in the **northern hemisphere**, spends more of the day facing towards the Sun than facing away from it. When days are longer, the Earth receives more **energy** from the Sun, and the weather is hotter. In **winter** this part of the Earth spends more of the day facing away from the Sun than towards it. It receives less energy, and the weather is colder.

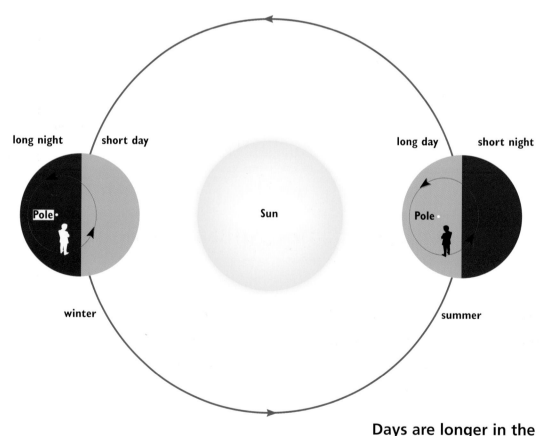

Days are longer in the summer than in the winter.

The height of the Sun

It also gets hotter in the summer because the Sun rises higher in the sky. This too is an effect caused by the Earth leaning on its axis. In summer, when the Sun rises high in the sky, the Sun's energy shines directly on the Earth. The Earth's surface gets lots of strong sunshine and **temperatures** are warm. In winter, when the Sun is lower in the sky, its energy is spread out over a larger area of the Earth's surface. It gets less sunshine and the temperature is colder.

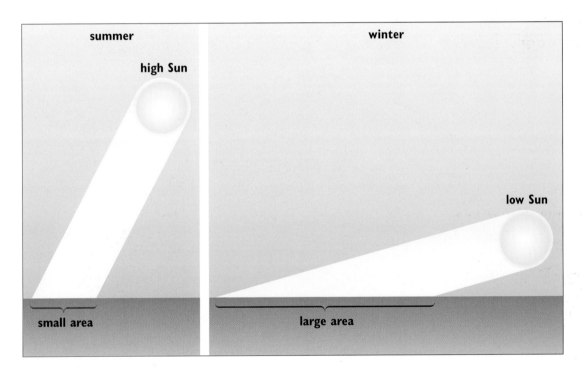

The **midday** Sun appears much higher in the sky in the summer than in the winter. When the Sun is lower, its energy is spread over a greater area – we get less of it, and the weather is colder.

The four seasons

Winter

In **winter**, the **midday** Sun is low in the sky. It is the time
of **year** when **temperatures** are usually at their lowest.
During the winter **months**, many trees are leafless and
some animals **hibernate**.

In some places snow is common in the
winter. In others it is much rarer.

In temperate areas, the appearance of daffodils marks the start of spring.

Spring

As the Earth continues its journey around the Sun, the **days** rapidly become longer, and the Sun rises higher in the sky. Little by little it starts to get warmer and **spring** begins. The buds on trees start to open, and new leaves appear. Birds lay their eggs, which hatch a few weeks later.

Summer

In the **summer** the days are at their longest, and the midday Sun is at its highest. Crops in the fields begin to ripen and young birds leave their nests.

Autumn

In the **autumn** the days quickly start to get shorter. The Sun does not rise so high in the sky, and the temperature begins to fall. Wild animals prepare themselves for the winter that will follow. The leaves of **deciduous trees** change colour and fall to the ground.

The length of our day

The length of our **day** depends on where we are and the time of **year**. On the **Equator**, every day of the year has almost equal amounts of **daytime** and **night-time**.

The further north or south of the Equator you are, the greater the difference between the amount of daytime in the **summer** and the amount of daytime in the **winter**.

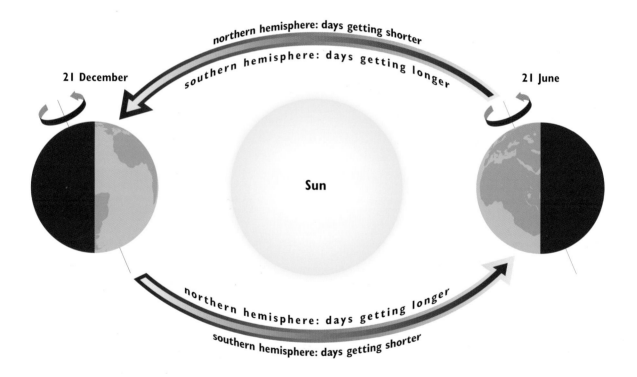

northern hemisphere: days getting shorter

southern hemisphere: days getting longer

21 December

21 June

Sun

northern hemisphere: days getting longer

southern hemisphere: days getting shorter

The length of our days changes as the Earth orbits the Sun.

The path of the Sun at different times of the year from London. It moves in a similar way in the USA and most of Europe.

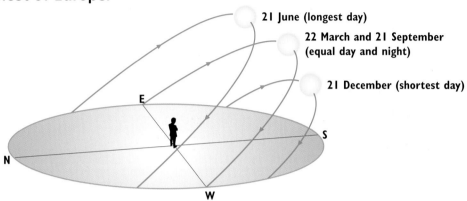

21 June (longest day)

22 March and 21 September (equal day and night)

21 December (shortest day)

The longest and shortest days

The **longest** and **shortest days** of the year occur in June and December. The amount of daylight increases each day between the shortest and the longest day. It then starts to decrease again. Roughly half-way between the two, we get more or less equal amounts of daytime and night-time.

length of day	approximate date	
	northern hemisphere (USA, UK)	southern hemisphere (Australia)
longest day	21 June	21 December
shortest day	21 December	21 June
equal day and night	22 September and 21 March	21 March and 22 September

The seasons in the Arctic and Antarctic

The land of the midnight Sun

In the **Arctic** and **Antarctic** circles, around the North and South Poles, there are long periods of unbroken darkness during the **winter**. In the **summer**, the Sun is still in the sky at midnight. There are long periods of continuous daylight. At the Poles, there is about half a **year** of continuous **night-time** followed by half a year of uninterrupted **daytime**. The number of **days** of each gets less as you move away from the Poles.

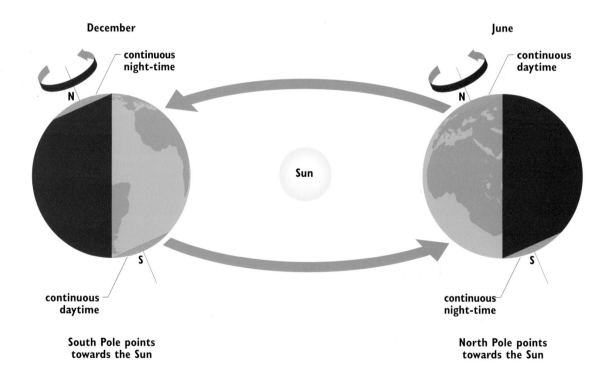

The land of the midnight Sun.

The circling polar Sun

At the Poles, the Sun moves round and round the sky at virtually the same height from one day to the next. It moves in a spiral. At the North Pole, it spirals continuously upwards until about 21 June. It then starts to spiral downwards again.

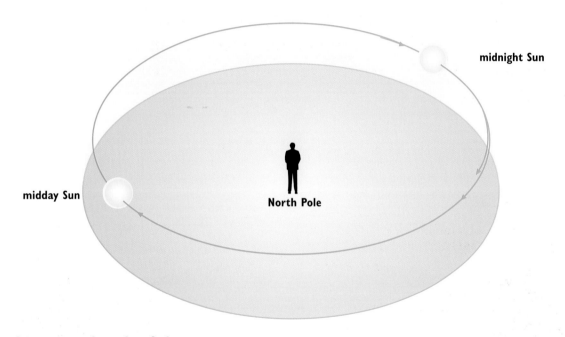

The upward path of the Sun at the North Pole in May.

The South Pole

At the South Pole the average temperature in December (in the summer) is minus 28° Celsius – colder than an ordinary freezer! Even so, it is 30° Celsius higher than the average temperature in June (in the winter), which is minus 58° Celsius.

The seasons near the Equator

The absence of seasons

The four seasons, **spring**, **summer**, **autumn** and **winter**, don't occur near the **Equator**. There is very little difference in temperature from one **month** of the **year** to the next. This is because each **day** is about the same length and the **midday** Sun is always high in the sky.

location		average temperature (°Celsius)	
		highest month	lowest month
[world map with Equator, dot on London]	London		
[world map with Equator, dot on Singapore]	Singapore		
[world map with Equator, dot on Sydney]	Sydney		

Rainy and dry seasons

In some places in the **tropics**, there is a dry and a rainy season. Part of the year is drier than normal, and part of the year is wetter. In other parts of the tropics, the rain falls more evenly throughout the year. The type of **climate** is influenced by the heating and cooling of the nearby land and oceans.

In the tropical rainforest, rain normally falls throughout the year.

height of midday Sun		*amount of daytime and night-time*	
highest	lowest	**longest day**	**shortest day**

Deciduous and evergreen trees

In the **tropics**, trees usually keep their leaves all through the **year**. Trees like this are called **evergreen trees**. Many of them have broad (wide) leaves. Beyond the tropics, there is usually a mixture of evergreen and **deciduous trees**. Deciduous trees normally lose all their leaves in the **autumn**, and grow new ones in the **spring**.

Autumn colours

The leaves of deciduous trees change colour before they fall to the ground in the autumn. The colour they turn depends on the type of tree. Some turn red. Others turn yellow or brown. The brightness of the colours is affected by the **summer** and autumn weather. New England in the USA is famous for its autumn colours.

The leaves of deciduous trees change colour before they are lost in autumn.

Evergreens in cold countries

The evergreen trees found in very cold places are usually **conifers**. Their leaves look like thin spiky needles. Although evergreens with broad leaves are often able to survive in the warmer **winters** in the UK, most are unable to survive the colder winters of the northern USA and Canada.

Woodland plants

Plants need light to grow. The ground in deciduous woodlands receives most light in the early spring when the trees have no leaves. This is when many woodland plants flower. In the summer, when there is a leaf **canopy** overhead, it is darker. Many woodland plants die back, surviving beneath the ground until growth starts again in the autumn.

Bluebells are woodland flowers. They flower in late spring.

Hibernation and migration

Hibernation

In the **winter** there is less food around for wild animals. Some mammals survive the cold winters and the reduction in food supply by **hibernating**. In the **autumn**, when food supplies are plentiful, they fatten themselves up and build up an **energy** store. When they hibernate they find a cosy place to settle for the winter. Their body **temperature** and heart-rate drops. They use energy at a slower rate, and are able to use their stored energy to live through the winter. To an outsider, they look as though they are asleep.

Dormice hibernate in the winter.

Migration

Some birds fly to a warmer country for the winter. This is called **migration**. Swallows, for example, spend the **summer** in northern Europe and the winter thousands of kilometres away in Africa, where it is warmer.

Fur colour and length

In the winter, when it is colder, mammals – for example cats – grow more and longer hair. In the summer, when it is warmer, they lose hair. This is called **moulting**. The colour of the fur of some mammals also changes with the seasons. This helps them to stay **camouflaged** as the landscape around them changes.

Stoats (in winter they are called called ermine) have brown fur in the summer, but white fur in the winter.

23

The seasons on other planets

Most of the planets have seasons. The more a planet leans on its **axis**, the greater the difference between its **summer** and **winter**. The planet that leans the most is Uranus. It is almost lying on its side. The planet that leans the least is Mercury. Mars and Earth both lean at about the same angle.

Uranus spins on its side, causing a big difference between its summers and winters. The blue-green colour is caused by methane gas in its atmosphere.

planet	tilt of axis (°)
Mercury	0
Venus	3
Earth	23
Mars	25
Jupiter	3
Saturn	27
Uranus	82
Neptune	28
Pluto	56

Surface temperatures

Many other factors also affect the **climate** and weather patterns on the planets. These include the amount and type of **atmosphere** and the distance from the Sun. In general, the further a planet is from the Sun, the colder its surface **temperature**.

Small planets have less **gravity** and less atmosphere than larger ones. Mercury, the smallest of the inner planets, has almost no atmosphere. Venus is about the same size as Earth and has an atmosphere made up mainly of carbon dioxide. Carbon dioxide is a greenhouse gas. This means that it traps the Sun's **energy** and makes the planet hotter.

The surface of Venus is permanently covered in clouds.

As a result, the surface temperature on Venus is higher than on Mercury, even though it is further from the Sun. Mercury does not lean on its axis. All its days are the same length, and there are no seasons.

What if...?

... the Earth was closer to the Sun?

If the Earth was closer to the Sun, we would still get the seasons, but it would be hotter. The Earth would **orbit** the Sun more quickly. Our **years** would be shorter, and so too would each of our seasons.

If we were close enough to the Sun, it would be too warm for water to freeze in the **winter**. The ice-caps of the **Arctic** and **Antarctic** would not have formed and the sea levels would be higher. If we were closer still, it would be too hot for life as we know it to exist.

If the Earth was closer to the Sun, the ice-caps would not exist.

If the Earth didn't lean, there would be no deciduous trees. Trees would keep their leaves throughout the year because the **temperature** would be about the same in December as in June.

... the Earth didn't lean?

If the Earth didn't lean we wouldn't get our seasons. And if we didn't have the seasons, we probably wouldn't measure time in years either. Our longest unit of time would be the **month**. The length of each month is based on the time it takes for the Moon to orbit the Earth.

If there were no seasons, there would be no **deciduous trees**. All the trees would be **evergreens**.

If the Earth didn't lean, the **midday** Sun would always reach the same height in the sky. Each **day** would be much like any other day. Every day would have virtually equal amounts of **daytime** and **night-time**. The further away from the **Equator** you were, the cooler it would be.

27

Factfile

Long school holidays in the **summer** are a hangover from the **days** when children helped to collect the harvest.

The highest **temperature** ever recorded (in the shade) on the Earth's surface was 58° Celsius. The lowest was minus 89.2° Celsius.

In Verkhoyansk in Russia, the difference between the highest recorded summer temperature and the lowest recorded **winter** temperature is 105° Celsius. This is greater than the difference in temperature between freezing and boiling water.

In Murmansk, the largest Russian town inside the **Arctic** Circle, the Sun doesn't set for about 62 days in a row in the summer.

Arctic ground squirrels **hibernate** for nine **months** of the year.

Arctic ground squirrel.

The coldest place where people live all through the year is the village of Oymyakon in Russia, where the temperature has fallen below minus 70° Celsius.

Nearly one-tenth of the Earth's land is permanently covered in ice. It stays frozen even in the summer months.

Around 21 March and 22 September, the **midday** Sun passes directly overhead at the **Equator**.

The seasons on Mars last roughly twice as long as those on Earth. Mars is further from the Sun, so it takes longer to complete each orbit.

Once a tree has been cut down, its age can be worked out by counting the number of tree rings – one for each **year** of its life. The rings are formed because trees grow at different rates in different seasons.

Garden plants which are able to survive the cold weather and frosts in winter are called hardy plants.

The body temperature of snakes and other reptiles is higher in the summer than in the winter.

Tree rings.

Glossary

Antarctic   the part of the Earth near the South Pole

Arctic   the part of the Earth near the North Pole

atmosphere   a layer of gases that surrounds a planet. A planet's atmosphere affects its temparature and weather.

autumn   the season between summer and winter

axis   an imaginary line passing through the centre of a planet from the North to the South pole, around which the planet spins

camouflage   to blend in with the surrounding area, often by changing colour

canopy   a covering of something

climate   the general type of weather and temperatures that a place experiences

conifer   a tree like a pine or fir tree that is evergreen and has needles and cones

day   a length of time based on the time it takes for the Earth to spin round once on its axis

daytime   the time between sunrise and sunset

deciduous tree   a tree that loses all its leaves in the autumn and grows new ones in the spring

energy   what it takes to heat something up or to make it move

Equator   an imaginary line that separates the Earth's northern and southern hemispheres

evergreen tree   a tree that keeps its leaves throughout the year

gravity   a force that attracts objects to each other. The Earth's gravity gives us our weight.

hibernate   to spend the winter in an inactive state

longest day   the day in the year with the most hours and minutes of daytime

midday   the time when the Sun reaches its highest point of the day

migrate   to move from one place to another

month   a length of time based on the time it takes for the Moon to orbit the Earth once

moulting   the shedding of hair in the spring and summer

night-time   the time between sunset and sunrise

northern hemisphere   the half of the Earth north of the Equator – the top half of a globe

orbit   the path of a planet around the Sun or a moon around a planet

shortest day   the day in the year with the fewest hours and minutes of daytime

southern hemisphere   the half of the Earth south of the Equator – the bottom half of a globe

spring   the season between winter and summer

summer   the hottest part of the year when the days are longest and the Sun rises highest in the sky

temperature   how hot or cold something is

tropics   the part of the Earth near the Equator

winter   the coldest part of the year when the days are shortest and the Sun is always low in the sky

year   a length of time based on the time taken for the Earth to orbit the Sun once and for the cycle of seasons to repeat itself. A normal calendar year has 365 days. A leap year has 366 days.

Index